simple

gifts

▼ style ▼

simple

gifts

▼ style ▼

DOROTHY WOOD

Photographs by Lucinda Symons

WATSON-GUPTILL PUBLICATIONS/NEW YORK

Acknowledgments

Many thanks to the following for supplying furniture and settings:

Nordic Style, 109 Lots Road, London, SW10 ORN. Tel: 0171 351 1755

Decorative Living, 55 New Kings Road, SW6 4SE. Tel: 0171 736 5623

Summerhill & Bishop, 100 Portland Road, London W11. Tel: 0171 221 4566

The Classic Chair Co, Old Imperial Laundry, SW11. Tel: 0171 622 4274

Damask, Broxholme Hoe, New Kings Road, SW6. Tel: 0171 731 3553

Joanna Wood, 48a Pimlico Road, London, SW1. Tel: 0171 730 5064

Published by MQ Publications, Ltd.
254-258 Goswell Road, London EC1V 7EB

First published in the United States in 1998
by Watson-Guptill Publications,
a division of BPI Communications, Inc.
1515 Broadway, New York, NY 10036

Series Editor: Ljiljana Ortolja-Baird
Editor: Simona Hill
Designer: Bet Ayer
Photographer: Lucinda Symons
Stylists: Clare Louise Hunt and Fanny Ward

Library of Congress Catalog Card Number: 98-60300

ISBN: 0-8230-4803-9

Printed in Italy

1 2 3 4 5 6 7 8 9/06 05 04 03 02 01 00 99 98

contents

introduction

Simple Gifts Style is for those of us who enjoy making simple and beautiful projects and who like to experiment with lots of different crafts. Nothing is more satisfying than making a gift for a friend or relative knowing that it will be appreciated all the more for the trouble and thought you have taken to produce it. Everyone loves to receive a handmade gift and most of us appreciate the planning, effort and time involved in producing a hand-crafted item. With this in mind I have designed a range of timeless classic projects – the kind of luxury items which we may not purchase for our-selves, but which we always appreciate. I have kept each project fairly sim-ple so that a beginner to any of the crafts I have included could tackle any of the 20 projects without being daunted by the size of the commitment or the time it will take to complete. Knowing that there is nothing worse than losing interest halfway through a project and feeling guilty that we have purchased expensive materials with no alternative use, I deliberately kept the projects small-scale so that they can be made quickly and easily.

It would be impossible to produce a book with a gift to suit every person for every occasion, so I have kept my project choices general, hoping to appeal to a wide audience, and introducing enough different craft skills for you to be able to adapt each project or technique to suit the recipient of your gift. The four chapters, Soft and Sensual, Garden Lover, Pen and Paper and All that Sparkles contain a

selection of exquisite gifts, many of which I have no doubt you would enjoy making for yourself. People who love exquisite fabrics, who enjoy being pampered and like to be surrounded by beautiful things would cherish any of the soft and sensual ideas. A garden lover does not necessar-ily need to have a huge garden, it could be a friend with a tiny patio or even just a few house plants on the kitchen windowsill. Someone who

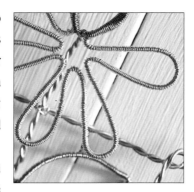

enjoys their home surroundings and likes to entertain would appreciate the exquisite designs in All that Sparkles. The Pen and Paper chapter includes a crackle-glazed stencilled letter rack, a selection of gift wrap ideas, pressed flower gift bags, a nubuck pencil case, a glasses case and a handmade paper notebook.

The projects are simple and elegant in design, straightforward in construction and made of materials that are readily accessible. When time is at a premium, saving time and equipment are important considerations. I have avoided using special tools other than those you might have at home or can buy from the local hardware or department store. Despite their appearance, the projects are not

expensive to make, since the scale of the projects means that the quantities used are not large, keeping the overall cost at a reasonable level. Top quality natural fabrics such as silk organza, Swiss organdy and Irish linen may seem prohibitive when bought by the yard but they are usually wide and you may only need to buy a small quantity.

You may not be familiar with all the crafts and techniques used in the book, but I believe people who enjoy making things are inherently good with their hands and pick up new skills with ease. Your enjoyment of sewing or painting, for example, may lead you to try one of the many other crafts I have included such as ribbon embroidery, appliqué, wirework, stencilling, foil craft, stamping, floral art or a wide variety of painting techniques. The projects are designed to inspire confidence. There are no particular artistic skills involved, it is more a case of following a recipe.

Even if some of the crafts are new to you, the step-by-step instructions have been carefully written to make them easy to follow. I suggest you try out any unfamiliar technique before beginning the real thing. For example, before starting work on the linen cushion, I practiced with the pear stencil on a scrap of fabric until I was comfortable with the technique. A trial run on a scrap

piece of linen ensured that the paint was the right consistency, the colors were accurate and the pears looked realistic. This initial experimentation only takes a short time but is worthwhile to ensure that the final piece is of a high standard.

The fabric projects require only basic sewing skills used for dressmaking, such as French seams as well as basic embroidery stitches such as the chain and buttonhole stitch. The instructions are easy to follow and will produce an impressively tailored item. Following the instructions exactly, being adequately prepared and trying not to rush always make for a better quality article. Using best quality, 100% natural materials will help preserve the life of the project ensuring that it will last and look good

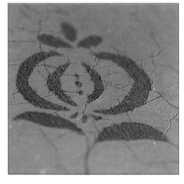

for years to come. For the fringed parison between using silk and beautifully and the depth of color is bouncy fabric: it would be difficult to crisp, clean lines of these scarves ite work on the drawn-thread bag is of the bleached linen – no other fabwell. There are no patterns or of the designs – even the beads

organza scarves, there is no com- polyester organza. The silk handles unmatched. Polyester organza is a work French seams or achieve the with polyester. Likewise, the exquisbalanced with the weight and body ric starches or holds its shape so stripes to detract from the simplicity have been chosen for their subtlety.

Wherever possible I have used natural materials for the project base: the papers chosen are simple – traditional waxed sandwich wrapping, plain tissue, fine corrugated card or handmade paper. I have also included a beautiful selection of fruit and foliage. There are beautiful leaves and pretty

pressed flowers as well as unusual dried plant material such as pomegranates and litchi nuts. For decoration I have included many new and modern products: crackle varnish, iron-on fusible webbing, acrylic gesso, neoprene foam and an assortment of varnishes.

Simple Gifts Style contains projects that will be a joy to make, a pleasure to give and a delight to receive.

▶ 9

soft and sensual

▶ 11

Soft and Sensual is a chapter of timeless classic gifts – six romantic gifts that are stylish and elegant, but practical too!

When making these projects, choose the best quality fabrics available: luxurious chenille velvet for the chenille drawstring bags, silk organza for the fringed organza scarves, soft organdy for the organdy potpourri sachets, Irish linen for the drawn-thread bag and pure new wool for the ribbon embroidery throw.

The stitching involved in making up these projects is simple and well within the capabilities of anyone with access to a sewing machine. I have chosen to use classic dressmaking techniques such as French seams and hand-stitched hems for these beautiful gifts, since it is attention to detail that makes the difference to the quality of your workmanship and ultimately the finished product. The decoration on this group of projects is more time consuming and requires some knowledge of basic embroidery stitches. (Instructions can be found in any basic embroidery manual).

Choose exotic mother of pearl buttons and beautiful silk cord to complete the organdy potpourri bags and use pure silk thread with exquisite translucent frosted beads for the fringed organza scarves.

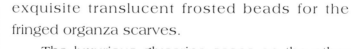

The luxurious glycerine soaps on the other hand are so quick and easy. These are definitely a last-minute gift idea! A citrus-based perfume will complement the orange, lemon and lime zest to provide the essential finishing touch. Once you've mastered the technique, experiment with different combinations.

SOFT AND SENSUAL

drawn·thread
bag

▼

I have been passionate about drawn-thread work for many years. This traditional embroidery technique is usually worked on white linen so that the simple background does not detract from the beautiful stitching. The appearance is of panels of fabric held together or "floating" between fine lacy stitching. This technique is not difficult to master, although counting and accuracy when withdrawing the threads is essential. I have chosen a simple basic stitch for beginners and suggest you choose an even-weave linen suitable for cross-stitch. The threads on even-weave linen are quite distinct, making it easy to cut across the threads and count them into groups. Once the embroidery is complete, the linen can be heavily starched so that the bag will hold its shape.

Detail showing the twisted chain stitch pulling the bars of threads together.

fringed organza
scarves

Accessories change an outfit, dressing it up or down as the occasion requires, breathing new life into favorite clothes. To add the final touches to a special evening outift I have designed an immaculately tailored organza scarf with a heavy silk fringe.

Irridescent organza, shown here in rich jewel colors, is woven using different colored warp (vertical) and weft (horizontal) threads. As the light catches the different threads. the colors shimmer. For a thick, lush fringe, I used pure silk embroidery threads packed close together and have given the choice of finishing your scarf fringe in three different ways – with beading, thick silk tassels or a beaded web.

Detail of the beaded fringe.

organdy
potpourri sachets

▼

These potpourri sachets deserve to be on display rather than hidden away in the linen closet. This classically simple design in cool, crisp organdy has been tailored with French seams. Each of the three bags is made to the same basic design but all are finished in a slightly different way to give them each an individual style. One is finished with a gentle smooth scalloped edge, another is fastened with two symmetrically placed mother of pearl buttons and the third is fastened with a silk cord couched into a heart. This project requires some basic sewing skills.

Beautiful silk cord adds the finishing touches to the scalloped edge of this potpourri sachet.

molded glycerine soap blocks

▼

These translucent citrus soaps are so easy to make – the basic clear soap compound can even be melted in the microwave! To the basic ingredient add your choice of scent, color and appropriate natural ingredients such as zest of limes, oranges and lemons to make the finished item more interesting. Choose the addition carefully and tailor it to suit the recipient. If you choose to add oatmeal it becomes a simple body scrub so beware when using coarse materials.

The soap can be made to any shape and size using jelly and chocolate molds or improvise using milk cartons and yogurt cups. Large soap shapes are easy to cut with a sharp knife once set.

SOFT AND SENSUAL

ribbon embroidery throw

Ribbon embroidery is such an easy technique to master, it is ideal for newcomers to embroidery, since the design is filled in quickly and the result is more instant than traditional embroidery. This soft, fleecy wool is embroidered with delicate pastel silk ribbons in shades of blue and pink. The ribbon embroidery flowers are worked using just two simple stitches – lazy daisy stitch for the petals and sepals with French knots for the centers. I have chosen a simple grid pattern so that the throw can be made to any size. The edges are bound with loosely woven linen; substitute satin ribbon if the throw is a gift for a baby.

Detail of a daisy made using lazy daisy stitch with a French knot center.

chenille drawstring bags

▼

From time to time I buy a gift for a friend or relative –
perhaps some pretty handmade soap or a small piece
of jewelery I've found in an antique shop and some-
how it seems rather small and insubstantial when I
start to wrap it. My solution is to make a special bag
for the gift. These chenille drawstring bags are made
from two fabric rectangles so they can easily be
scaled up to make a luxurious bag for shoes or lin-
gerie. Personalize the bag by stitching a monogram or
a pretty flower motif on one side. The cord and tassels are handmade from an exquisite "silk" embroidery thread that matches the silk lining and contrasts
beautifully with the soft, pastel chenille velvet.

▶ 27

Close-up detail of the silk
cord and tassel wrapped with
gold thread.

garden lover

This is the chapter for those of us with friends who love to putter around in the garden – unusual copper foil tags shaped like leaves on which to write the name of a plant; beautiful terra-cotta pots stamped and painted to match interior decor; a rose covered wire-framed storage basket covered in scrim; a practical wirework hook rack on which to hang those important keys or small garden tools; and a soft plump cushion on which to nap outdoors when the hard work of pruning and weeding is over.

I have designed five gifts that any garden lover would be delighted to receive and which are a pleasure to make. Each uses a different craft skill from sewing, stencilling, painting, wirework and foil craft. The botanical linen cushion is decorated with a simple stencilled pear and with buttons to match. The raw linen is ideal for use outdoors since it washes beautifully. The charming rose basket makes an excellent holder for small garden tools. The ribbon roses can be adapted to suit a multitude of projects from hats to clothes and curtain tie backs. Decorate plant pots with an easy paint technique that will transform plain terra cotta instantly. Several simple stamped pots can be completed in a morning. Tinted acrylic gesso dries almost immediately and is ready for varnishing in under an hour.

Wirework and foil craft are two popular techniques. Both materials are readily available in craft stores and require only basic tools such as pliers. The stunning appearance of the copper foil leaves belies the simplicity of the undertaking. Rubbings of real leaves give the exact shape and indicate where to draw the veins and fine details. Wire is a versatile medium to work with, since it is easy to sculpt and the results are amazing. The twisted wire hook rack uses wire which is pliable enough to mold with your hands, only requiring the use of pliers to form tight bends.

GARDEN LOVER

twisted wire
hook rack

▼

I designed this twisted galvanized wire hook rack with a dual purpose – to be attractive enough to be on display, and to be sturdy enough to hold small tools in one place. Galvanized wire is a cheap, flexible material, soft enough to be bent by hand but strong enough to hold weight.

Draw a flower shape on paper as a guide for where to bend the wire. Each flower is fashioned from a single piece of galvanized wire, then wrapped in fine silver or copper wire before being attached to the rack framework.

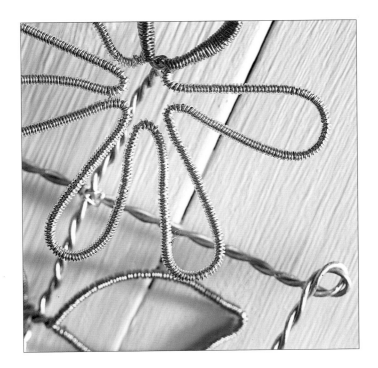

Detail of the simple flower petal shapes wrapped with fine wire.

rose storage basket

Gardener's storage boxes are usually quite plain and totally utilitarian so I thought it would be fun to decorate these mesh and wire-framed stacking boxes with handmade silk ribbon roses.

Ribbon roses are very easy to make. Once the ribbon has been wrapped around the stem and secured, twist the center of the rose into a tight bud and mold the wire edge of the ribbon into petal shapes. All that remains is the addition of silk leaves to make a realistic rose.

Close-up of a silk rose and leaf.

stamped flower pots

I love to see a group of old terra-cotta pots filled with geraniums or petunias on the patio in the summer. Indoors, pots painted with pale pastel shades are appealing, especially when planted with delicate flowers such as cyclamen and African violets.

The pots are first painted with acrylic gesso – a plaster-based paint used by artists to paint their canvases. It covers the porous surface of terra cotta very well and is easily tinted with acrylic paints. The checkerboard pattern is then stamped onto the pots with gold acrylic paint.

Detail of the checkerboard design on the pot surface.

botanical stencilled cushion

This linen cushion has been stencilled with an attractive group of ripe pears. The paint dries quickly and the different colors can be painted one on top of the other right away. Once you have cut the stencil, filling in the shape takes no time at all. The stencil paint must be set when dry using the heat of a hot iron and should be left for several days before washing.

The cushion design is easy to make up since only very basic straight line stitching is required.

Detail showing the red and yellow shading on the fruit.

copper foil
garden tags

▼

I often plant seeds or cuttings and then forget where and when I planted them. These exquisite garden tags have proved to be the answer. The veined leaf is purely decorative and a second small leaf is embossed with the plant name. The sturdy bamboo pole is stuck into the soil giving you an attractive ornament to look at until the seeds or cuttings begin to grow. The leaves are remarkably detailed because they are traced from a rubbing taken from a real leaf.

Close-up of the detailed veins.

pen and paper

▶ 43

K eeping up with old friends and new acquaintances, and exchanging gifts are simple pleasures which link all the projects in this chapter: a nubuck pencil case for holding pens; the stencilled letter holder to keep important correspondence; handmade paper notebooks in which to record noteable events; pressed flower gift bags that make beautiful packaging; and wrapping paper and gift tags for those special gift ideas.

This chapter includes the introduction of a new craft technique – old fashioned waxed paper, more usually associated with the kitchen than with stylish craft projects has been made into beautiful gift bags. Pressed flowers

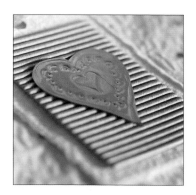

are sealed between two layers
iron. The sheets are then neatly fold-
wrapping paper. To make the hand-
flowers to the front cover. The iron-
icate flowers. Plan ahead, if the book
wedding guest list it would be a nice
from the bridal bouquet on the front.
ety of papers and card that are torn
assembled. The tags can be deco-

when the wax is melted with a cool
ed into a bag, or could be left as
made paper notebook, fuse pressed
on fusible webbing preserves the del-
is to record a special event such as a
touch to include foliage and flowers
The gift tags are made from a vari-
or cut into shape before being
rated with a variety of objects – tiny

feathers, interesting seed heads or dried leaves.

For the pencil and glasses cases I have chosen nubuck – a beautiful smooth, soft suede leather which is easy to stitch using a domestic sewing machine. The pencil case is the more challenging of the two projects because of its curvy shape. The stencilled letter holder is beautifully decorated with an attractive pomegranate stencil and is aged with crackle varnish.

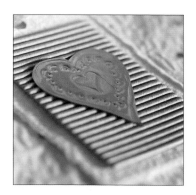

pressed flower
gift bags

▼

During the spring and summer months I like to press flowers from the garden with great intentions of using them to make something during the winter. Without fail they have always remained in the press until the following year, when I start again! But now I've found a beautiful way of using them in all their glory.

These exquisite bags are made from the traditional waxed paper which is available from grocery stores. The pressed flowers are arranged between two sheets and sealed using a cool iron. When the paper layers cool it can be used as wrapping paper or folded as shown to make into a bag.

Detail of an old-fashioned violet and fern leaves.

handmade paper notebooks

There are many occasions when you might want to record something in a special book – guests at a wedding, mementos from a holiday or plants in your garden. These attractive notebooks can be made in any shape or size, just add extra sheets of paper as required.

We are spoiled with the many choices of wonderful handmade paper available from all over the world. I chose a slightly mottled paper to show off the pressed ivy and acer leaves and used thick paper for the inside. The books are bound with natural hemp string.

Pick your selection of leaves when they are at their peak in the garden. The iron-on fusible webbing preserves the appearance of the leaf although the colors will become muted with time.

stencilled letter holder

This sturdy letter rack has all the style and markings of a bygone era, but is made using medium density particleboard which is painted and stencilled, then distressed with ageing techniques. Crackle varnish is applied to the dry surface and then dried fast with the heat of a hairdryer. Practice first on spare pieces of painted wood to achieve the desired degree of crackle. The distressed effect is achieved by rubbing burnt sienna oil paint over the crackled surface. The excess paint is rubbed away, leaving a fine coating in the cracked surface.

Detail of the gold stencilled pomegranate and initials.

pencil case
and glasses case

▼

How many of us keep our pencils in a plastic holder and glasses in the rather boring case they came in for lack of a more attractive alternative? I have designed two simple, stylish nubuck leather cases in an unusual color combination.

The pencil case has tabs to hold when opening the zipper and a neat little tassel to finish it off. The glasses case is a simpler shape but styled to coordinate with a similar tassel fastening. Nubuck is relatively easy to stitch on a conventional sewing machine because it is so soft, but be careful since mistakes cannot be unpicked without leaving a line of unsightly holes.

Accurate workmanship is
essential for these nubuck cases.

all that sparkles

b e a d e d
f r u i t

These exquisite beaded fruit can grace the table for months on end. All that is required is a blow from a hairdryer from time to time to remove the dust. Make a small group of a single fruit, such as pears, or make one of each type to fill a glass dish.

Silk fruits are available from florist's suppliers and craft stores. I prefer to use them rather than polystyrene foam because they are a better shape and have realistic stalks which add the finishing touch. The technique is easy, just thread a small seed bead onto a short beading pin, add a sequin then press the pin into the fruit shape.

Detail of a pear and an orange.

b e a d e d
s l i p p e r s

▼

While it would not be practical to stitch seed beads onto a relatively solid foundation such as a slipper, it is possible to add decorations by making them separately and applying them in completed shapes to the front of the slipper.

Simply thread the beads onto pieces of gold wire to make individual motifs, then bend the wire into your choice of shape such as a coil or heart and arrange it on the front of the slipper. Then sew the beaded wires to the shoe. Choose cut glass beads in colors to match your favorite accessories to make a real impression.

Detail of beaded spirals.

pomegranate
pyramid

In winter, when fresh flowers are scarce or expensive, this gilded table decoration will make a dramatic centerpiece for a dinner party or special occasion. Buy a selection of different-sized dried pomegranates so that they decrease in size from the bottom of the pyramid to the top. Look out for other dried plant material in the same deep red, such as litchi nuts which will contrast very well with the pale green moss. Although you can buy cone-shaped oasis, I prefer to fit blocks in the pot and cut it to the exact shape and size required. If you do not own a glue gun, drill two small holes close together in the base of the dried materials and thread a length of wire through, then push the wire ends into the oasis block.

Pomegranate with gold
paint effect.

gilded frames

▼

Traditional gilding with gold leaf was always a job for the "experts" but nowadays Dutch metal leaf is readily available to the amateur. This paint product produces professional results quickly. Dutch metal leaf is sold in packets and is available in different metallic shades and can be used to create a variety of finishes.

My first frame shows the beauty of the gold leaf when applied over a dark red base, while my second frame has been distressed and aged. My third choice, which also has an antique finish is coated with crackle varnish and dried with a hairdryer. Paint the frame in dark red before gilding to seal the wood and add warmth to the final finish.

Detail of the three finishes on the different picture frames.

ALL THAT SPARKLES

putting it together

▶ 71

S*imple Gifts Style* is designed to introduce you to many different crafts. It is not necessary to be an expert in any one skill because the techniques and instructions are simple to follow. To avoid costly mistakes, practice on scrap material first to familiarize yourself with the procedure and gain the necessary confidence to produce a good result. Just like following a recipe, read and understand the instructions first and then collect together all your tools and materials before you start a project.

Some projects such as the beaded slippers and beaded fruit require little manual skill, but an eye for balance and proportion when choosing the colors of the beads will improve the final result. The paper projects require accuracy; use a ruler and measure carefully to ensure corners are square before cutting. The sewing projects can all be made entirely by hand, but a sewing machine is neater and will make light work of the mostly straight seams. The embroidery projects require knowledge of some basic stitches.

The list of equipment needed for making projects is basic – pliers and wire cutters for the twisted wire hook rack and beaded slippers, paint brushes for the stamped flower pots and gilded frames, scissors, iron and sewing kit for the fabric projects and a hole punch for the handmade paper note-

books. The success of the projects depends on your choice of colors and materials as well as the quality of the workmanship. Think ahead, and if necessary order fabric from a fabric store or mail-order company. Try not to compromise and select only the best quality materials. Although initially more expensive, the reward for paying a little more will be a lovely gift, thoughtfully and carefully made.

PUTTING IT TOGETHER

drawn-thread bag

Delicate drawn-thread work is easier than it may appear. Once completed, the bag can be starched and pressed to hold its shape.

MATERIALS
◆ *Even-weave Zweigart linen –*
22 x 12in/56 x 31cm
◆ *White flower thread*
◆ *Sewing kit*
◆ *Spray starch*
◆ *White cord for the handle –*
20in/50cm

1 Measure 1¾in/4.5cm from one long edge (the bag top). Working with one thread at a time, carefully remove ten horizontal threads across the full width of linen.

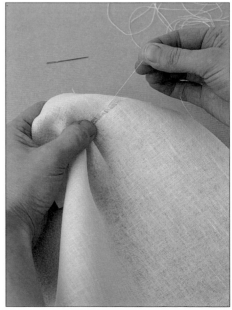

2 Fold the linen in half across the width. Machine stitch an accurate ½in/1cm side seam.

3 Trim the side seam allowance above the drawn threads to ¼in/0.5cm. Zigzag the rest of the side seam close to the stitching and trim.

4 Turn under ¼in/0.75cm at the top raw edge. Fold again so that the folded edge aligns with the top of the drawn threads. Baste.

5 With the seam at one side, baste a 2⅜in/6cm square in the center of the bag front, 2⅜in/6cm below the drawn threads. Snip through ten horizontal threads in the middle of one side of the square. Draw out the ten threads carefully – there should be exactly 84 vertical threads. Repeat on all sides.

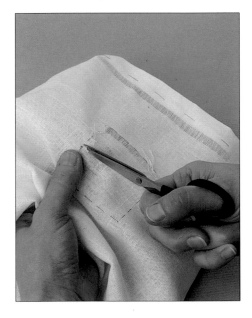

6 Hem stitch the linen at each side of the drawn threads. Sew the threads into

bundles of four and stitch three threads deep into the linen. The hem stitch will make bars of threads to resemble a ladder pattern.

7 Carefully work buttonhole stitch around the corners at the outside edge. Trim the excess threads close to the buttonhole stitch.

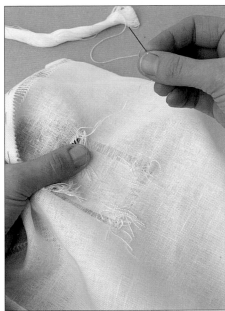

8 Beginning in the middle of the buttonhole stitch, work twisted chain stitch sewing the ladder threads into bundles of two. At the corner take the flower thread through the buttonhole stitch on the wrong side and continue along the next side.

9 Stitch a diagonal thread across each corner and sew the thread ends in on the reverse side.

10 Work twisted chain stitch along the drawn-thread work at the top of the bag.

11 Spray both sides of the bag with starch and press using a medium hot clean iron. Repeat the process until the linen is quite stiff.

12 Turn the bag inside out. Stitch the bottom seam. Zigzag close to the stitching and trim the excess.

13 To make a flat-bottom bag, open out the corners and line the bag bottom seam up with the side seam or fold line. Stitch across the seams through both layers 1⅜in/3.5cm from the corner.

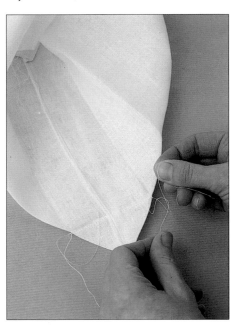

14 Turn the bag right side out. Press a neat crease up the side seam working from each bottom corner. Lay the bag flat, then tuck the side seams in and press flat.

15 Cut the cord in half and oversew one piece to each side of the bag to make two handles.

fringed organza scarves

76 ◀

Irridescent organza is one of the most lux-urious and beautiful fabrics to work with.

MATERIALS
◆ *45in/115cm wide silk organza:*
20in/50cm of red, blue and green
◆ *Kreinik mori silk embroidery thread to*
match the scarf color
◆ *A selection of beads (optional)*
◆ *Sewing kit*
◆ *Sleeve board*
◆ *Tapestry needle*

1 To square-up the edges of the fabric, pull a thread close to each raw edge to reveal a straight line. Cut across from selvedge to selvedge. Cut the fabric in half along a pulled thread to make two long panels.

2 Place the panels wrong sides togeth-er. Stitch the long side seams taking a ¼in/0.5cm seam. Trim the seam to ⅛in/0.3cm.

3 Press the seams open on a sleeve board and turn the scarf right side out.

4 Press flat, then stitch the long side seams again using a ¼in/0.5cm seam. Press the French seams flat.

5 Stitch the ends of the scarf using a ¼in/0.5cm seam, leaving a small gap in the middle of one end for turning.

6 Clip across the corners and turn through. Ease out the corners and press the scarf flat.

7 Cut four skeins of silk mori thread into 16in/40cm lengths. Double-up each strand and thread the two cut ends into the needle.

8 Bring the needle up through the edge of the scarf and take it back through the loop of thread before pulling tight. Continue along the edge of the scarf sewing the threads of the fringe quite close together.

BASIC FRINGE

1 Count the threads into eight. If there are too few in the last bundle either take out some threads across the width of the scarf or if possible add some more.

2 Make a knot in each group. Slip a tapestry needle into the loop of the knot and use the needle to work the loose knot up to the top of the fringe. Holding the needle where you want the knot to be, pull the end of the threads until the knot is formed (see picture next column).

BEADED FRINGE

1 Divide the threads, this time into a group of eight threads which are knotted as before, then two unknotted threads for the beads.

2 Using a fine tapestry needle, thread the beads onto the single pair of threads. End each string of beads with one with a small center hole. Tie the threads in an overhand knot to secure.

BEADED NET FRINGE

1 Tie 36 bundles of threads across the fringe. Split the bundles for the second row and thread a bead onto every second bundle. Tie a knot as before on the ones in between.

2 Split the bundles again and tie a third row of knots to secure the beads and complete the fringe. Trim the thread ends neatly and evenly.

NET FRINGE

1 Knot the fringe into bundles as described in the basic fringe.

2 For the second row, split each bundle in half and tie adjacent half bundles together using the tapestry needle technique to guide the knot to the right position before pulling tight. Leave the half bundles at each end and carry down to the next row.

3 Continue splitting the bundles until the net fringe is the desired depth. The scarf shown on page 76 has six rows of knots. Trim the ends evenly.

organdy potpourri sachets

▼

The main instructions given are for the square flap bag with the heart appliqué. Each bag is made from the same basic design and instructions for dealing with different flaps are given on page 79.

MATERIALS

◆ 45in/115cm wide organdy: 1/3yd/30cm
◆ Paper for the template
◆ Pencil
◆ Sewing kit
◆ White silk embroidery thread
◆ Iron-on fusible webbing
◆ Silk cord: 20in/50cm for the scalloped and pointed edge bag
◆ Quilting pencil

• Use a 1cm/1/2in seam throughout.

1 Make a paper pattern for the square flap bag 20¼ x 9¼in/53.5 x 25.5cm.

2 Fold the organdy in half crossways and pin the pattern along the straight grain, keeping the pins within the seam allowance. Cut out through both layers and keep them pinned together.

3 On each long edge, measure 3½in/9cm from one end. Mark the point with colored thread in each seam allowance. Machine stitch around the end of the organdy between the colored threads to form the bag flap. Stitch the other short end.

4 Trim the seam allowance to ⅛in/0.3cm. Clip off the corners and turn through. (For the scalloped bag see page 79.)

5 Press the seams flat. Fold the short straight edge up to meet the start of the square flap and press the fold. Put aside.

6 Iron the fusible webbing to one side of a scrap of organdy following the manufacturer's instructions.

7 Make a template of the heart and cut out. Draw around it three times on the paper side of the web and cut each out. Remove the backing paper.

8 Position the hearts on the bag front, between the two layers of organdy and just below the flap. Press to fuse the hearts in place.

9 Pin the side seams and stitch ¼in/0.5cm from the raw edge. Trim the seam allowance to ⅛in/0.3cm and press open as far as possible.

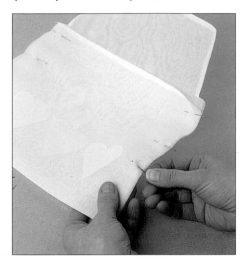

10 Turn the bag through and press flat. Stitch the side seams again ¼in/0.5cm from the edge. Sew in the thread ends. Turn the bag through and press.

11 Work running stitch around the edge of the hearts. Tie the ends off on the reverse side.

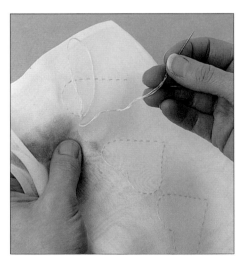

12 Mark the position of the buttons on the flap and work two buttonholes. Sew buttons in the corresponding position on the bag front.

BRAIDWORK FOR THE ENVELOPE FLAP BAG

1 Make a paper pattern as for the square flap bag 22 x 9¼in/56 x 25.5cm. Trace the template provided and pin it so that the point is in the center of one short end. Cut out.

2 Trace the braidwork design directly onto the organdy using a quilting pencil.

3 Fold the cord in two and pin around the lines leaving a small loop to fasten the bag at the point.

4 Oversew the cord, stitching through the top thickness of organdy. Stitch the loop securely.

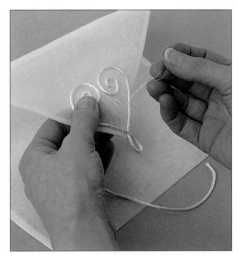

5 Oversew the cord several times at the end of the design and snip the cord close to the stitches.

6 Sew a toggle or button on the bag in the corresponding position.

SCALLOP EDGE BAG

1 Make a paper pattern for the scallop flap bag 22 x 9¼in/56 x 23.5cm. Trace the template provided and pin it so that the scallop is at the short end. Cut out.

2 When trimming the seam allowance of the scalloped edge, clip small notches out of the curves to ease turning through and make the curves lie flat.

3 Fold the cord in half and oversew under the center of the flap on the bag front. Trim the ends to the required length and wrap with thread to prevent them from fraying.

4 Sew a small loop with several strands of thread in the middle of the scallop edge, just large enough to pass the silk cord through.

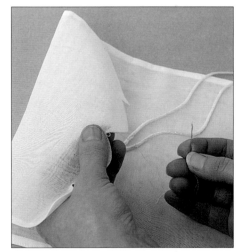

5 Work buttonhole stitch around the thread loop and sew in the ends.

molded glycerine soap blocks

▼

Handmade soaps are a luxury. Translucent glycerine soap compound is available from craft suppliers and you can add a few drops of your favorite perfume to scent the soap. Food coloring is a suitable alternative to cosmetic colors but add just one drop at a time as they are much stronger.

MATERIALS
◆ *Glycerine soap compound –*
  ¹⁄₂lb/250gm of each color
◆ *Cosmetic colors or food coloring*
◆ *Cosmetic scent*
◆ *Citrus fruits*
◆ *Zester*
◆ *Heat-proof dish*
◆ *Double-boiler*
◆ *Grater*
◆ *Milk carton or similar container*

1 Grate the soap compound into a heatproof dish and place in a double-boiler until it melts. If using the microwave, heat at full power for only 10 seconds at a time before checking. Be careful as the soap melts quickly and will boil over and may even ignite if heated too long.

2 Remove the dish from the heat. Add a few drops of color as desired. Then add a few drops of scent and stir. Set aside.

3 Cut a carton down to 2in/5cm high.

4 Using a zester, cut thin strips of peel from a citrus fruit and drop into the base of the carton.

5 Reheat the soap compound if a skin has formed on the surface, then pour the liquid into the carton.

6 Use a toothpick to distribute the peel evenly and allow to cool before placing the carton in the refrigerator.

7 Once the soap has set (about one hour), it can be turned out. Ease the sides of the carton away from the soap and press the base of the carton until the soap drops out. Cut into four.

8 Make orange, lemon and lime colored soaps in the same way to complete the set.

r i b b o n   e m b r o i d e r y   t h r o w
▼

Ribbon embroidery is a simple but effective way to decorate a soft fleecy blanket or throw since only two stitches are used and the decoration is quick. The throw can be lined to cover the raw ends before attaching the linen border.

MATERIALS

◆ *Fleecy fabric for the blanket*
◆ *Embroidery ribbons – 2mm width in pastel colors*
◆ *7mm width – in pastel colors*
◆ *Open-weave linen*
◆ *Vanishing ink pen*
◆ *Ruler*
◆ *Sewing kit*

1 Cut the fabric to the required size and square-up the edges.

2 Fold the fabric in half and then in half again to find the center point. Mark the center point with pen. Measure every 5in/12cm along the fold lines, stopping about 5in/12cm from the raw edge. Fill in the grid of dots spaced every 5in/12cm (see picture next column).

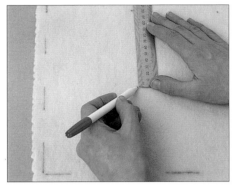

3 At each dot, work a lazy daisy stitch flower with five petals. Keep the petals short so that the flower looks full. Choose the colors randomly and avoid stitching two adjacent flowers in a similar color.

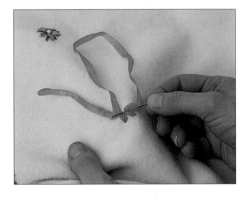

4 Work a lazy daisy stitch between each petal in a shade of green. Vary the green from flower to flower.

5 Work a French knot for the flower center using cream ribbon. Wind the needle round the needle three times before taking it through to the reverse side.

6 Cut four pieces of linen 5in/12cm wide and 4in/10cm longer than each side of the blanket. With right sides together, center the linen along each edge of the blanket 1½in/4cm from the raw edge.

7 Stitch the first piece of linen in place using a ½in/1cm seam, beginning and finishing 2in/5cm from the edge of the blanket. When sewing the second and subsequent pieces of linen, fold the previous piece out of the way and begin stitching at the same corner point, 2in/5cm from the edge.

8 Miter the corners on the right side and slipstitch in place. Trim the excess fabric.

9 Turn under ½in/1cm along the long edge of the linen. Fold over to the wrong side of the blanket as far as the stitching. Pin. Miter the corners on the wrong side and trim the excess fabric. Hem the linen to the machine stitching and slipstitch along the mitered edge to complete the throw.

chenille drawstring bags

▼

These exquisite bags can be made in any size as a make up holder, shoe bag or even a large and luxurious laundry bag. The method of construction is the same but larger bags would benefit from ready-made cord and tassels and for laundry bags a more practical fabric. Stitch a simple motif or initial in the bottom right-hand corner for decoration before sewing up the bag.

MATERIALS

◆ *Chenille velvet: 8in/20cm*
◆ *Habutai silk: 8in/20cm*
◆ *3 skeins of Marlitt thread*
◆ *Gold thread*
◆ *Sewing kit*
◆ *Bodkin*

1 Cut two pieces of chenille for the outside of the bag and two pieces of silk for the lining each 12 x 8in/30 x 20cm.

2 Place the chenille right sides together. Machine stitch down the long sides and across one short side. Press the side seams open as far as possible.

3 To make the bag bottom, open out the corners and match the bottom seam to the side seam. Measure 1¼in/3cm down the side seam from the point and pin. Machine stitch across the triangular point and turn through to the right side.

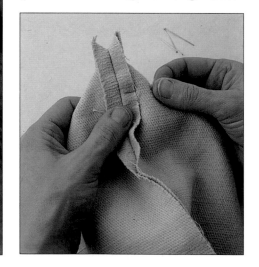

4 Make the lining in the same way, leaving a 2in/5cm gap along the short edge for turning. Press the side seams open.

5 Tuck the chenille bag inside the lining, with right sides together. Match the seams and pin the raw edges around the top. Machine stitch ½in/1cm from the top raw edge.

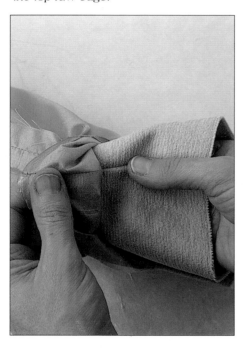

6 Turn right side out, then slipstitch the gap. Tuck the lining inside the bag. Press the top edge flat.

7 Machine stitch a casing for the cord around the bag 2¼ and 2¾in/6 and 7cm from the top edge. Snip into the stitching in the side seams between the two rows of channel stitching.

8 To make a cord with one skein of Marlitt thread, fold the cord in half and tie the ends to a door handle. Tuck a

pencil into the loop at the other end. Holding the thread taut, twist the pencil around and around until the cord is tightly twisted.

9 Remove the cord from the handle, fold the thread in half and tie the ends together. The two halves of the cord will automatically twist together. Run the cord between your finger and thumb to even out the twists. Cut the cord evenly in half and tie the ends to prevent them from unravelling.

10 Use a bodkin to thread one cord around the bag, through the casing from one side and back out of the same gap. Thread the second cord through from the other side.

11 Pull the two cords tight and tie a knot in each just below the bottom of the bag to form drawstring handles.

TO MAKE A TASSEL

1 Cut one piece of cardboard 3½in/9cm square.

2 To make a tassel, wrap a skein of Marlitt thread tightly around the center of the card, then snip the threads along one edge only.

3 Lay the threads out in a bundle on top of the cord ends, so that cut ends align.

4 Make one knot just below the midpoint. Tie a strong thread around just above the knot to secure the threads.

5 Ease the threads around the cord evenly and then let them drop down over the knot. Wrap gold thread around the tassel below the knot to form a "neck" and tie off. Sew in the ends. Make a second tassel to match the first and trim the ends evenly.

twisted wire hook rack

Silver and copper wire have been wrapped around a galvanized wire frame to create a strong hook rack sturdy enough to hang small garden tools on.

MATERIALS

◆ *1.65mm (16 gauge) galvanized wire*
◆ *0.6mm silver-plated jewelery wire*
◆ *0.6mm (24 gauge) copper jewelery wire*
◆ *Wire cutters*
◆ *Needle-nose pliers*
◆ *⅝in/1.5cm thick piece of plywood*
◆ *2 "C" clamps*
◆ *Hand drill*
◆ *Masking tape*

1 Cut a 2⅓yd/2m length of galvanized wire. Beginning 6in/15cm to one side of the center, bend the long end of the wire into five continuous petals. Use your hands for the softer curves and the pliers for the tight bends.

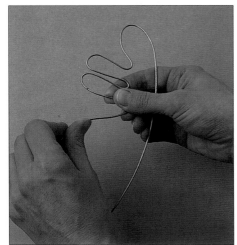

2 Bring the two ends together to make a rounder flowerhead using a double thickness of wire.

3 Secure the flowerhead upside down on the block of wood using a "C" clamp. Hold the galvanized wire halfway down each length and twist together to make a 3½in/9cm long stem.

4 Bend the wire to form a leaf on each side of the stem. Using pliers, twist each leaf around close to the stem.

5 Secure the stem with the "C" clamp again and continue twisting for another 3½–4in/9–10cm.

6 Bend the wire straight back up on both sides. About 2½in/6cm from the end of the stem form a small loop on one side for a screw. Wrap the other wire around the stem five or six times and snip both ends. Bend the end up to form a hook (see picture next column).

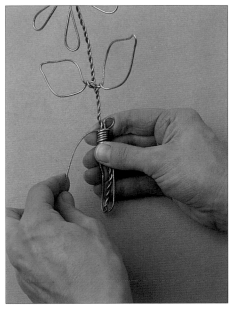

7 Wrap each flower petal with silver wire. Use 36in/90cm lengths of wire and begin in the middle, using one half of the wire for each side of the petal.

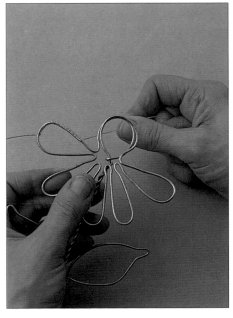

8 Wrap the flowerhead and leaves in the same way using a 40in/1m length of copper wire.

9 Snip the ends off on the reverse side once the flower is complete.

10 Cut a 2¼yd/2.5m length of galvanized wire and wrap the ends with masking tape. Put both ends into the chuck of the drill and tighten.

11 Hook the other end around a large nail secured into the block of wood. Turn the drill handle to twist the wire until it looks the same as the stem.

12 Bend a loop in the twisted wire about 10in/25cm from one end and another 3in/8cm away to make one end of the wire rack.

13 Bend the wire back up 14in/36cm along and make the other end to match.

14 Overlap the ends and find the center. Unravel the ends of the wire and twist one end on each side around to secure. Trim the ends.

15 Place the flowers on the wire rack. Wrap silver-plated wire round the stems where they cross the rack.

16 Screw or nail the rack to a wall using the loops at the base of each hook. If required, additional nails can be put in each of the corner loops.

17 If preferred, the wire flowers can be hung individually by attaching a wire loop to the back of the stem.

stamped flower pots

Plain terra-cotta pots have been transformed with subtle pastel paints and a simple checkerboard design. The distressed appearance is created by rough stamping in gold. These pots are suitable for outdoor use if painted with several coats of clear satin varnish.

MATERIALS
- *Terra-cotta garden pots*
- *Acrylic gesso*
- *Acrylic paints – black, purple, green, dark red, gold*
- *Paint brush*
- *Neoprene foam sheet*
- *Cardboard or empty thread reel*
- *Acrylic varnish*
- *Waxed paper*
- *Paper towel*

1 Mix a small amount of colored acrylic paint to gesso to achieve a pale pastel color. Add a small quantity of black to dull the color slightly. Paint the terracotta pot inside and out with two coats of tinted gesso, allowing it to dry between coats.

2 Cut a square of neoprene, ⅝in/1.5cm for a large pot and ⅜in/7mm for a small pot. Stick the neoprene to a square of thick cardboard and add a suitable handle such as a narrow thread reel or coiled cardboard.

3 Make a stamping pad by sandwiching a damp folded paper towel between two layers of waxed paper. This prevents the paint from drying too quickly.

4 Drop a small amount of paint onto the silicone paper and work it into a thin layer with the stamp. Try out some prints on a piece of scrap paper. You may have to roll the stamp from top to bottom and side to side to make a clean square print.

5 Print a square just under the rim of the pot, then print a square touching each bottom corner of the first row to create a checkerboard pattern.

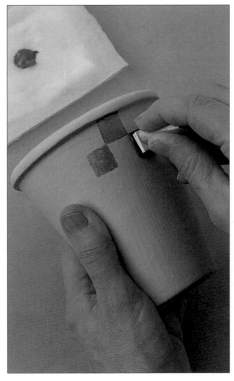

6 Work down the pot in a "v" shape. Overlap the corners slightly as you go down the pot to accommodate the curved sides. This is more pronounced in larger sizes (see picture next column).

7 Use the same stamp to print a gold band around the rim of the pot. Roll the stamp over the rim and stop the same distance inside the pot each time.

8 Once the paint is dry, apply two coats of clear varnish.

botanical stencilled cushion

▼

Stencilling is a quick and easy way to add a motif to a cushion. Build up layers of color gradually so that the paint does not bleed under the stencil. The stencil paints are set using a hot iron, allowing the cushion to be washed at a later date. Buy natural coordinating buttons to add a finishing touch to the border.

MATERIALS
◆ *54in/140cm wide raw linen – 20in/0.5m*
◆ *Stencil paper*
◆ *Tracing paper and black pen*
◆ *Craft knife and cutting board*
◆ *Spray mount*
◆ *Fabric stencil paints – green, red, yellow, white*
◆ *Stencil brush*
◆ *Sewing kit*
◆ *20 red, green and cream buttons in total*
◆ *12in/30cm cushion pad*

1 Wash the linen fabric to remove any finish and press while still damp.

2 Trace the pear template onto tracing paper using a black pen.

3 Cut four pieces of stencil paper large enough to fit over the design.

4 Place the tracing on a cutting mat and tape the stencil paper on top. Cut the central pear from the first piece of stencil paper. Cut the other two pears, the leaves and the stalks from separate pieces of stencil paper.

5 Apply spray mount on the wrong side of the stencils and leave to dry slightly.

6 Cut a 18in/45cm square of linen and fold in four to find the center point. Position the first pear stencil over the mid-point and press firmly to stick it to the linen.

7 Mix a pale yellow pear color from white, yellow and a touch of green fabric paint. Stencil the lefthand side of the pear. Add some white to some red paint and stencil the righthand side of the pear for definition.

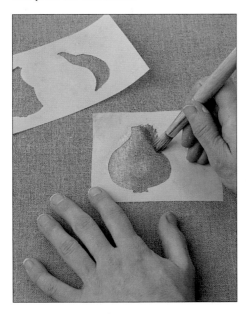

8 Shade the pear with darker yellow and red. Stencil some dark flecks of green with an almost dry brush and add highlights with white.

9 Peel off the first stencil and position the second carefully. Color the other pears in a similar way and lift off the stencil when complete.

10 Stencil a light shade of green on one side of the leaves and a darker shade on the other. Add shades and highlights to give the leaves more definition.

11 Finally stencil the stalks by mixing a brown from red, green and ochre yellow paint. Color the top of the stalks with red paint and add highlights down the side.

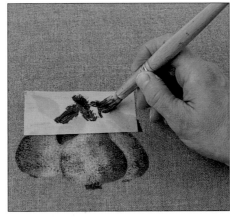

12 Once the paint has dried, set the stencil by pressing with a hot steam iron. Move the iron continuously for a few minutes and leave for at least 72 hours before washing.

13 Cut two pieces of linen each 12 x 18in/30 x 45cm for the back of the cushion. Turn under a ⅝in/1.5cm hem along one long edge of each piece and pin. Machine stitch close to the fold.

14 With right sides together, pin one piece along the top of the cushion and pin the other piece along the bottom so that the hems overlap in the middle. Machine stitch around all four sides ½in/1cm from the raw edges (see picture next column).

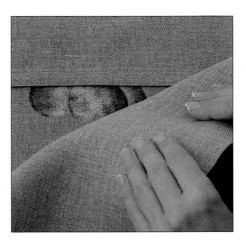

15 Trim the seams, cut across the corners and turn right side out. Roll the seams between your fingers and baste close to the edge.

16 Machine stitch 2in/5cm from the edge all the way around the cushion Reinforce the opening by stitching the side seams again.

17 Stitch a button every 2¾in/7cm all the way around the border edge of the cushion, alternating between red, green and cream buttons.

18 Insert the cushion pad to complete.

pressed flower gift bags

These beautiful bags are made from two sheets of waxed paper which are ironed together, sandwiching pressed flowers between the layers. Although quite sturdy once made, the wax paper is slippery, so practice folding plain paper first until you are confident with the technique of folding up the bag.

MATERIALS
- *Waxed sandwich wrapping paper*
- *A selection of pressed flowers and leaves*
- *Piece of cotton muslin*
- *Scissors*
- *Tweezers*
- *Iron*

- *Double-sided tape*
- *Hole punch*
- *Cord or organza ribbon for the handle*

1 Cut two pieces of waxed paper 8 x 12in/21 x 31cm for a small bag, 10 x 17in/26 x 44cm for a medium bag and 12 x 20½in/30 x 52cm for a large bag.

2 Using an ironing board covered with the piece of muslin for your surface, place one sheet of wax paper shiny side up. Arrange two or three large flowers on the paper, then fill in with smaller flowers.

3 Arrange small pieces of fern between the flowers facing in different directions. Fill in spaces with small leaves.

4 Once you are satisfied with the arrangement, place the second piece of waxed paper on top shiny side down.

5 Press the sheet with a cool iron to melt the wax. Allow to cool.

6 Fold the paper in half widthways – this fold is the center of the bag bottom. Fingerpress the fold, then open out. It may be easier to define the bag bottom, at this stage.

7 At each side of the centerfold, make a fold 1⅛in/2.75cm away, across the width of the bag.

8 For the bag top, fold over ¾–1½in/2–4cm (dependent upon the size of the bag) at each short end. Fingerpress the fold, then open out.

9 For the bag sides, fold over 2¼in/5.5cm along one long edge. Fold the flap back on itself, exactly in half. Open out the second fold.

10 With the bag bottom positioned vertically in front of you and the flap away from you, pick up the top righthand flap and make a diagonal pleat in the paper so that the fold line defining the center of the flap aligns with the centerfold of the bag bottom.

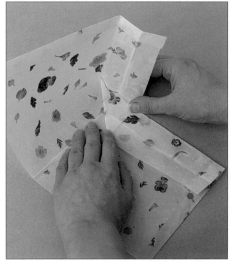

11 Make a diagonal crease on the lower-righthand side flap, so that the bag sides stand upright and there is a neat triangular flap in the righthand corner of the bottom of the bag.

12 Repeat the process along the other long edge, making sure that the overlap is facing in the same direction on both sides of the bag.

13 Put a ¾in/2cm piece of double-sided tape above the top crease between the layers of both side panels and stick the layers together.

14 Tuck the bag top flap inside the bag and re-crease the side seams.

15 Punch two holes with a hole punch on each side of the bag.

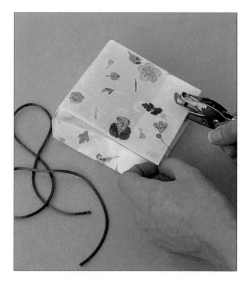

16 Insert a length of cord through the holes. Tie a knot in one end, adjust the length and tie a knot at the other end so that the knots are on the inside of the bag. Trim evenly.

gift tags and wrapping paper

Three simple techniques will show you how to transform plain tissue paper into an attractively decorated paper which can be used for wrapping special gifts. Gold wire, copper foil motifs, corrugated card and buttons are used to make attractive gift tags.

MATERIALS
- ◆ *Tissue paper*
- ◆ *Water spray*
- ◆ *Acrylic paints in a variety of colors*
- ◆ *Bleach*
- ◆ *Fine paint brush*
- ◆ *Toothbrush*
- ◆ *Handmade paper*
- ◆ *Corrugated card*
- ◆ *Raffia string*
- ◆ *All-purpose glue*
- ◆ *Superglue*
- ◆ *Ruler*

SWIRL DECORATION

1 Place the tissue paper flat on the ironing board and spray lightly all over with water. Press the paper with a medium hot iron, lifting the iron to move it rather than dragging it across the paper.

2 Pour some bleach into a small container. Dip in a fine paint brush and wipe off the excess. Paint swirls over the whole surface taking care not to drip or splatter the bleach.

SPECKLED DECORATION

1 Cover a large area of floor with newspaper. Lay a sheet of wrinkled tissue paper in the middle.

2 Mix some acrylic paint to the consistency of light cream. Dip the bristles of the toothbrush in paint and shake off the excess.

3 Holding the brush clear of the edge of the paper, run your finger across the bristles to cause tiny droplets of paint to splatter over the paper.

4 Avoid holding the brush over the paper by turning the paper as required. Use two or three different colors to build up the depth of color on the paper.

POLKA DOT DECORATION

1 Using a plain piece of tissue paper, paint tiny dots over the entire surface. Allow to dry.

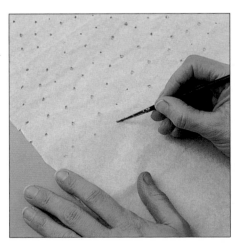

2 Spray the reverse side with water and press as before.

GIFT TAGS

Handmade paper and corrugated cardboard can be used to make a variety of gift tags in different shapes and sizes. Use some of the techniques shown in other projects, such as the pressed flower gift bags and the copper garden tags and the coiled wire heart to make attractive decorations or simply add buttons, feathers or beads.

1 Tear the handmade paper against the side of a ruler to produce a rough edge.

2 Cut the corrugated card along a groove and at right angles to keep it exactly square.

3 Punch a hole in the top of the flat gift tag or near the fold of the inside back panel on a folded tag.

4 Stick the wire, copper or button in place using superglue and stick the paper with an all-purpose glue.

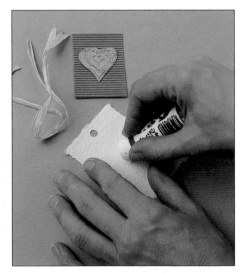

5 Add a natural raffia loop to finish.

▶ 95

handmade paper notebooks

▼

The leaves on the front of these notebooks have been bonded between two layers of iron-on fusible webbing which adheres the leaves to the surface and provides a protective layer on top. The same technique can be used to apply flowers, threads and feathers.

96 ◀

MATERIALS
◆ *Mountboard or thick cardboard*
◆ *White tissue paper*
◆ *Mottled handmade paper*
◆ *Spray mount*
◆ *Pressed leaves*
◆ *Iron-on fusible webbing*

◆ *Hemp string*
◆ *Watercolor paper*
◆ *Hole punch*
◆ *Craft knife and cutting mat*
◆ *Awl*
◆ *Ruler*
◆ *Gum tape*

1 Cut four pieces of cardboard 6 x 9in/ 15 x 23cm and trim off a 1¼in /3cm wide strip from one end of each. Set these strips aside.

2 Spray spray mount on one side of each large piece and stick together to make up a double thickness for the front and back covers.

3 Place the strips parallel with the main panels, ¼in/0.5cm away, and stick together with gum tape. Turn the panels over and stick a strip of tape down the other side of the join.

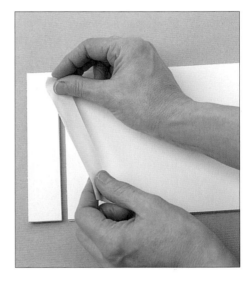

4 Cut the tissue paper ⅝in/1.5cm larger than the cover panels. Spray spray mount on one side of the tissue paper, center the paper over the panels and stick in place. Miter the corners neatly and stick the overlap on the reverse side.

5 Place the mottled paper over the front panel and crease to mark the edges of the cover. Cut a piece of fusible web-

bing to fit just inside the crease lines. Iron in position. Peel off the backing paper and arrange the leaves on top.

6 Place a second sheet of fusible web-bing on top of the leaves and press with a hot iron. Allow to cool before peeling off the backing paper.

7 Spray the reverse side of the mottled paper with spray mount. Place the paper over the front cover, lining the creases up with the edge of the panel. Smooth the paper out towards the

edges to stick and trim ¾in/2cm larger than the panel.

8 Turn the panel over and fold in the overlap, mitering the corners neatly.

9 Cut a piece of mottled paper to fit ¼in/0.5cm in from the edges. Stick on the inside of the cover. Cover the back of the notebook in the same way, but without the leaves.

10 Mark the position of the holes in the middle of the end strips. Punch through the cardboard with an awl or similar sharp tool.

11 For the leaves of the book, cut pieces of watercolor paper to fit inside the covers. Mark the position of the holes and punch two or three sheets at a time with a hole punch.

▶ 97

12 Thread natural hemp string through the holes in the back cover and add the sheets of paper. Finally thread the string through the holes in the front cover and tie in a bow.

stencilled letter holder

Individualize a blank letter rack with antique-effect paint techniques and stencilled initials.

MATERIALS
- *Unfinished letter rack*
- *Mint-green matte latex paint*
- *Stencil paper and glue*
- *Craft knife and cutting mat*
- *Black pen*
- *Fine paint brush*
- *Spray mount*
- *Gold stencil paint and stencil brush*
- *Scraps of felt*
- *Two-step crackle varnish*
- *Burnt sienna oil paint*
- *Hairdryer*
- *Gold metallic paste*
- *Matte polyurethane varnish*

1 Remove the center panel of the letter rack for ease of handling, then apply two coats of mint-green paint. Avoid painting the edges of the middle panel which fit into the side grooves. Sand lightly when completely dry.

2 Enlarge the initials on a photocopier to an appropriate size and draw over the outlines with a black pen.

3 Trace the pomegranates and outline with a black pen. Place the tracings on a cutting mat and tape a piece of stencil paper on top of each. Using a craft knife, cut out the larger shapes. The fine lines on the letters and tiny details such as the stems and dots on the small pomegranates can be added later by hand.

4 Apply spray mount to the back side of the stencils and allow to dry. Position the letter stencil in the middle of the front panel and press firmly to stick.

5 Apply the gold paint carefully with the stencil brush, building up the color slowly to avoid the paint seeping under the stencil.

6 Peel off the stencil and complete the letters in pencil. Use a very fine brush to go over the lines with gold paint.

7 Stick the pomegranate stencil on the back panel of the letter rack in the same way and apply the gold paint as before. Peel off the stencil and add the fine details with a fine paint brush.

8 Stencil a small pomegranate on each side of the initials. Don't paint the stems but paint in the other fine details.

9 Paint the front surface of the middle panel first, and then the letter holder, with an even coat of ageing varnish.

10 Leave the varnish for about 1 1/2–2 hours until it is almost dry. The timing depends on the temperature and humidity of the room. The varnish will dry more quickly in a warmer, drier environment.

11 Paint the middle panel of the letter rack with crackling varnish. Use your finger to gently smooth the surface. This removes the brush strokes, ensuring that the varnish is absolutely flat and that no areas have been missed.

12 Dry the panel with a hairdryer held 8–12in/20–30cm away. Stop once the cracks begin to form. If you are satisfied with the cracking apply the crackling varnish to the letter rack in the same way and dry with the hairdryer. If the cracking doesn't work satisfactorily wash off the varnish and repeat allowing the varnish longer to dry.

13 Once all the surfaces of the letter rack have been crackle varnished, leave to dry overnight. Use a piece of paper towel to rub oil paint over the whole surface. Wipe off the excess and buff with a soft cloth leaving the dark oil paint showing in the cracks.

14 Insert the middle panel. Dip your finger in gold metallic paste and wipe along the bottom rim and top edges of the letter rack. Paint all surfaces with two coats of matte polyurethane varnish. Cut a piece of felt to fit the bottom of the rack and glue in position to finish.

gilded frames

▼

Gold can be applied to plain wooden frames by gilding or painting. Both methods require undercoating with a dark red paint to give the gold a rich, warm appearance.

MATERIALS

◆ *Plain wood frame*
◆ *Dark red acrylic paint*
◆ *Gold leaf*
◆ *Gold size*
◆ *Shellac*
◆ *Gold paint*
◆ *Two-step crackling varnish*
◆ *Burnt sienna oil paint*
◆ *Hairdryer*
◆ *Paint brushes and cotton balls*
◆ *Steel wool and paper towels*

1 Paint the frames with two coats of dark red paint and allow to dry.

GOLD LEAF FRAME

2 Brush gold size on the frame, covering the surface and allow to dry until tacky (about 20 minutes depending on the environment). Wash and dry your hands to remove all traces of gold size.

3 Cut the gold leaf sheets in half. Lift the pieces one at a time onto the frame and smooth out with your finger. Overlap the pieces by 1/8in/0.2cm.

4 Stick the leaf flat over the frame and snip into the corners before smoothing down on to the inside rim.

5 Brush the frame gently with a soft paint brush in the direction of the overlaps and collect the tiny pieces of gold leaf. Rub these tiny pieces into any gaps and smooth down with cotton balls.

6 Paint the frame with a coat of shellac.

DISTRESSED GOLD LEAF FRAME
1 Brush gold size over the frame along the grain, leaving small gaps between the strokes.

2 Leave to dry for 20 minutes until tacky, then apply the gold leaf. Use torn and tiny pieces to bridge gaps.

3 When dry, brush lightly in the direction of the overlaps. Rub some areas with fine steel wool to remove some of the gold leaf and distress the edges.

4 Paint the frame with a coat of shellac.

CRACKLE VARNISH FRAME
1 Paint the frame with two coats of gold paint and allow to dry.

2 Paint the frame with a coat of ageing varnish and leave for 1½–2 hours until almost dry. (The length of time will depend on the environment – warm, dry conditions will speed up the process.)

3 Apply a coat of crackling varnish. Wipe over the varnish with a finger until it is completely smooth. This process ensures that no area has been missed and that all the brush strokes have been removed.

4 Use a hairdryer to speed the drying process. Hold it about 8–12in/20–30cm from the surface and stop as soon as the cracks begin to form.

5 Allow the varnish to dry overnight. Apply burnt sienna oil paint over the whole surface and remove the excess with a paper towel. Buff the frame with a soft cloth.

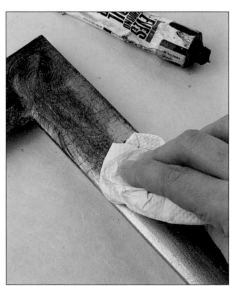

6 Paint the frame with a coat of shellac to complete.

templates

▼

A B C D E F G H I J K L M
N O P Q R S T U V W X Y Z

stencilled letter holder

enlarge as appropriate

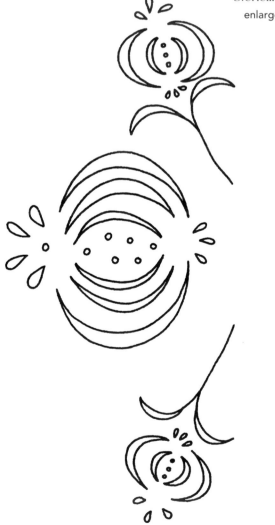

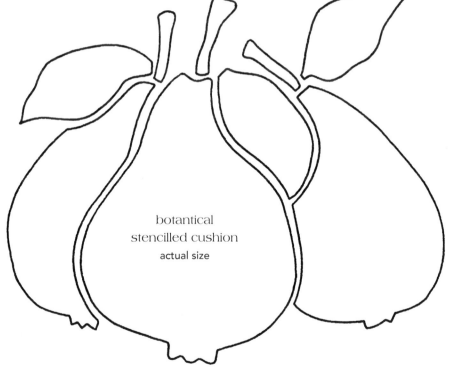

botantical
stencilled cushion

actual size

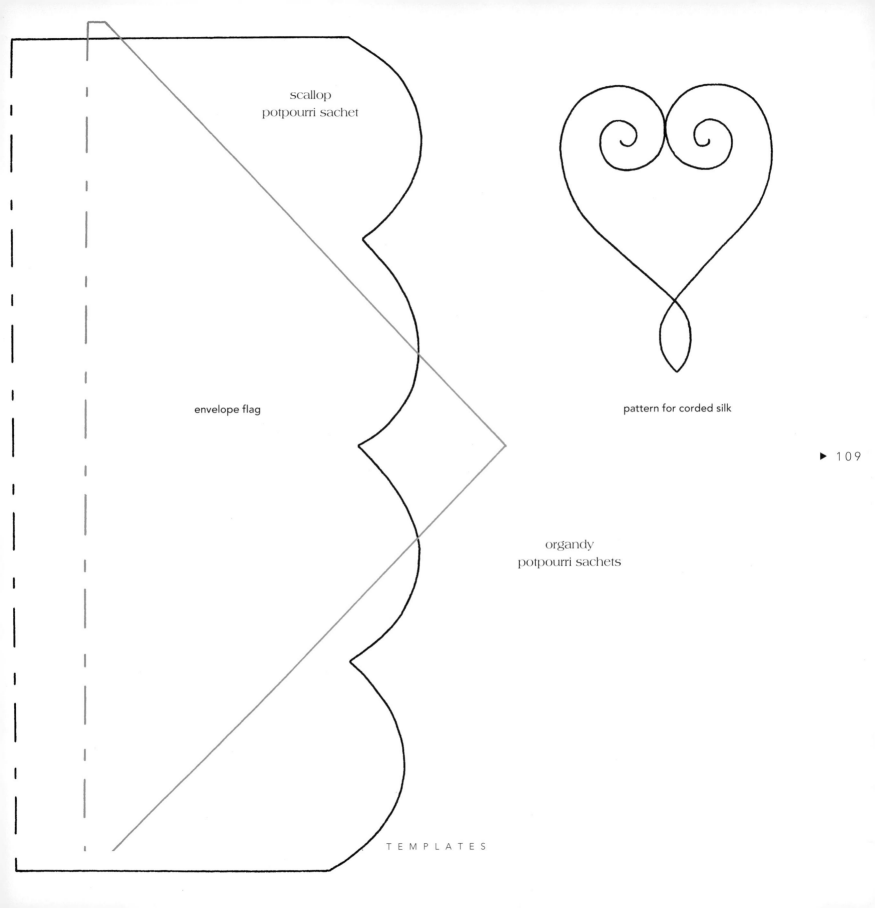

scallop
potpourri sachet

envelope flag

organdy
potpourri sachets

pattern for corded silk

► 109

TEMPLATES

pencil case

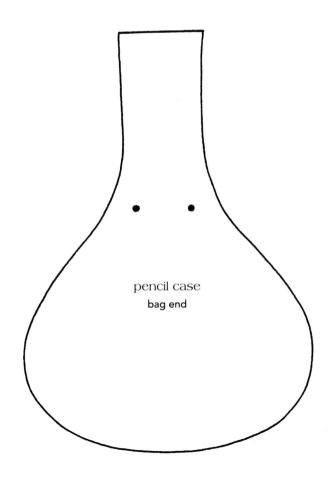

pencil case
bag end

index